SHOULD CHRISTIANS DRINK WINE AND ALCOHOL?

Ben David Sinclair

CONTENTS

Introduction

The King James Version of the Bible (KJV) mentions the word "wine" no fewer than two hundred thirty-one times. Wine is discussed, or mentioned, in at least forty-six of the sixty-six books of the Bible. It is clearly a widespread, biblical topic. It is well known that famous biblical characters like Noah, David, and the disciples drank what the Bible calls "wine." It is also well known that famous, church leaders today enjoy wine or beer. This booklet will explain and define the biblical term "wine" and will then answer the title question: "Should Christians Drink Wine and Alcohol?"

The Controversy Surrounding Wine

The drinking of wine has been a controversial issue among Christians for generations. Some believe that Christians should never drink wine. Many of these Christians believe that drinking an alcoholic beverage is sinful. They practice total abstinence from the drinking of alcohol. On the other end of the spectrum one can find some Christians who believe that total abstinence from alcohol is sinful.[1]

---

[1] In his book, *The Radical Reformission* (Grand Rapids, MI: Zondervan, 2004), Mark Driscoll includes a chapter entitled "The Sin of Light Beer" (139), in which he argues that Christians should drink strong beer rather than light beer. He goes on to testify that his early position of total abstinence was a "sin" (146). Driscoll's position that total abstinence is "sin" is based on opinion and bad logic. It cannot be supported biblically.

The most common position held by professing Christians around the world today is somewhere in between the two extreme positions of "drinking alcohol is sin" and "abstinence is sin." This middle ground is called "drinking in moderation." Most churchgoers that I have talked with hold to the opinion that Christians can drink wine in moderation. The common rule of thumb for many Christians is "Drink, but don't get drunk." In reality, the controversy surrounding wine has only two arguable positions. Either Christians should never drink alcoholic beverages (abstinence) or they can drink them, but should control or limit their intake in order to prevent drunkenness (moderation).

The Bible is very clear that **drunkenness is sin**. The Bible specifically commands in Ephesians 5:18, "And be not drunk with wine" (see also Galatians 5:21 and 1 Corinthians 5:11).[2] First Corinthians 6:10 plainly states that drunkards shall not inherit the kingdom of God. Abstinence and moderation are the two positions at odds today in the modern controversy surrounding wine. I am not interested in the opinions of church leaders or denominations or in what the reformers of old and the big name preachers of today preach. I want to know what the Bible has to say about this issue. **God's Word is the authority for the disciples of Christ – not the words, traditions, or opinions of men.**

Two Essential Questions About Wine

The concept of wine brings different things to mind for different people. Today wine refers to "an alcoholic drink made from fermented grape juice."[3] However,

---

[2] Even Mark Driscoll, who claims that his first 30 years of total abstinence were "sin," teaches that drunkenness is sin.

[3] Google, "wine," Google Dictionary, accessed August 22, 2017, https://www.google.com/search?q=wine+definition&oq=wine+definition&aqs=chrome..69i57j0l5.3632j0j7&sourceid=chrome&ie=UTF-8.

this definition has only been assigned to wine in recent times. The Bible was not written in the 21st century, and the English KJV was translated back in the 17th century. Therefore, the first essential question to ask in a study of this controversy is "What is wine?"

What Is Wine?

Four hundred years ago, the word *wine* had a more general meaning than it does today. The first known English dictionary to include a definition for the word *wine* was published in 1658 (right around the time of the translation of the KJV).[4] It was called, "The New World of English Words," and was compiled by Edward Philips. Philips defined the word *wine* as "a Liquor made of the Juice of Grapes or other Fruits" [*sic*].[5] Once again, this definition highlights another word that has evolved to mean something completely different today. Today the word *liquor* refers to an "alcoholic drink, especially distilled spirits."[6] However, in the 17th and 18th centuries, the word liquor was defined as, "any Thing that is Liquid; Drink, Juice, Etc." [*sic*] (Exodus 22:29). In his book, *The Bible and Its Wines*, Charles Wesley Ewing cites four dictionaries published in the 1700s.[7] All of these dictionaries

---

[4] John Simpson, "The First Dictionaries of English," Oxford English Dictionary, accessed August 22, 2017, http://public.oed.com/aspects-of-english/english-in-time/the-first-dictionaries-of-english/.

[5] Edward Philips, "The New World of English Words," Internet Archive, accessed August 22, 2017, https://archive.org/stream/The_New_World_of_English_Words_Or_A_General_Dictionary#page/n707/mode/2up/search/wine.

[6] Google, "liquor," Google Dictionary, accessed August 22, 2017, https://www.google.com/search?q=liquor+definition&oq=liquor+definition&aqs=chrome.0.69i59j0l5.4590j0j7&sourceid=chrome&ie=UTF-8.

[7] The four dictionaries cited are Nathan Bailey's *New Universal English Dictionary of Words, and of Arts and Sciences* (1730), John Kersey's *Dictionarium Anglo-Brittannica, or A General English Dictionary* (1708), B. N. Defoe's *A Complete English Dictionary* (1735), and Benjamin Martin's *"Lingua Brittanica Reformata, or A New English Dictionary* (1748).

define wine generically as **the juice or liquid extracted from a grape or other fruit.**[8] Likewise, in the Bible, the word translated *wine* did not exclusively refer to alcoholic wine either, but rather the liquid or juice of grapes.

Prior to the 20th century, the only way one could determine if the words wine and liquor were alcoholic or nonalcoholic was by the context. The context of a word refers to the setting, circumstances, words or ideas surrounding that word which clarify its meaning. In fact, when Thomas Welch first produced his now famous Welch's grape juice, the 1869 label boldly advertised: "Dr. Welch's Unfermented Wine."[9] The context of the word wine in the Bible is just as vital. **Only the context can determine if wine is fermented or unfermented.**

Are There Different Kinds Of Wine In The Bible?

The second essential question that must be answered in this Bible study is "Are there different kinds of wine in the Bible?" There are two popular positions or answers to this question. They are called the one-wine position and the two-wine position. Nearly all those who believe that drinking in moderation is acceptable claim the one-wine theory. The one-wine theory teaches that, without exception, every time the word *wine* is read in the Bible it is referring to alcoholic wine of some degree or another.[10]

---

[8] Charles Wesley Ewing, *The Bible and Its Wines* (Indiana: National Prohibition Foundation, 1985), 1-2.

[9] Welch's, "Our History," Welchs.com, accessed August 22, 2017, http://www.welchs.com/about-us/our-story/our-history.

[10] D. F. Watson, "Wine," in *Dictionary of Jesus and the Gospels: A Compendium of Contemporary Biblical Scholarship*, ed. Joel B. Green and Scot McKnight (Downers Grove, IL: InterVarsity Press, 1992), 870. Ironically, the second edition of this dictionary (2013) states that, "three kinds of wine made from grapes were in use . . . (1) fermented wine . . . (2) new wine . . . made from unfermented grape juices . . . and (3) wine in which the process of fermentation had been stopped by boiling the unfermented grape juice" (page 993).

The logical conclusion of this theory leads its supporters to teach that God requested alcoholic wine as an offering from His people in the Old Testament, that Jesus made alcoholic wine at the wedding in Cana of Galilee, that He offered wine to His disciples at the last supper, and that the Apostle Paul instructed Timothy to drink alcohol for his stomach's sake.

The two-wine position maintains that there are perhaps several types of wine in the Bible, but that of these potential types of wine there are basically only two distinct categories - alcoholic wine and nonalcoholic wine. Both one-wine and two-wine supporters use evidence from four key arguments. Historical, grammatical, theological, and medical evidences are used by both moderate drinkers of alcohol and teetotalers.[11] The following points will evaluate the evidence.

Historical Evidence

The historical arguments for the one-wine position often begin with the claim that the majority of Christians in church history practiced moderate drinking of alcohol, and that the temperance movement was basically a modern innovation. This argument is completely irrelevant. As was stated earlier, the teachings and opinions of men and their activities mean nothing in light of Scriptural evidence. The title of this study does not ask what most people do or have done. This Bible study wants to answer the question, "Should Christians drink wine and alcohol?" This question can only be decided by biblical truth, not by historical consensus.

---

[11] The first three of these considerations were drawn from the introduction of Randy Jaeggli's book, *Christians and Alcohol: A Scriptural Case for Abstinence* (Greenville, SC: Bob Jones University Press, 2014). "Teetotalers" is a term used to describe people who never drink alcohol.

The historical argument for the one-wine position usually goes on to say that all wine in the Bible was alcoholic because the ancients had no way of preserving nonalcoholic juice in their hot, middle eastern climate. This argument is common, but completely false.

Fermentation is a process that occurs when microorganisms, such as yeasts or bacteria, transform sugars found inside grapes or must into ethanol also called alcohol.[12] The alcohol is the byproduct or toxic waste of the microorganism after consuming the sugars in the grape juice.[13] If bacteria can be denied access to the sugars in the grape juice, then fermentation will be prevented.

Pasteurization (the heating of food and drink until all bacteria are killed) is the most common method of preventing fermentation today, and is the exact method Welch used in 1869 to create "Dr. Welch's Unfermented Wine." What most one-wine theory proponents ignore, or do not know, is that the ancients also had means of preventing or delaying fermentation as well as preserving nonalcoholic wine or grape juice for multiple years.

At least four means were actually employed in biblical times to preserve

---

[12] Must is unfermented grape juice or grape juice intended for fermentation.

[13] Drinking the waste of microorganisms sounds neither healthy nor appetizing to this writer.

nonalcoholic grape juice. One means was **filtration** (Isaiah 25:6). "By filtration, the gluten or yeast is separated from the juice of the grape. Whilst the juice will pass through the filtering implements, the gluten will not, and, being thus separated, the necessary conditions of fermentation are destroyed."[14]

Fumigation was a second means employed by some in Bible times. Fumigation was accomplished by the fumes of sulfur or by adding a small amount of sulfur (found naturally in eggs) to the must.[15]

Cold storage was a third popular method. If the container and juice were prepared and sealed properly, unfermented wine could be kept "sweet" in bottles under a cool "spring," or "pond" for more than a year.[16]

The oldest surviving work of Latin prose is an agricultural manual written by the Roman senator named Cato the Elder. His *De Agri Cultura* was written about 160 BC. This manual contains an entire chapter on the "preparations and preservation of wines, olives, lentils, etc."[17] This chapter is extremely insightful to a historical study of how sweet, unfermented wines were prepared and preserved in Bible times. Cato describes the use of straining or filtering wine. He describes the use of cold storage so people could enjoy sweet wine throughout the entire year. Boiling wine was prescribed or mentioned eight times in this chapter and it seems clear that the sweet, unfermented wine was preferred to fermented alcoholic wine as a beverage. Vintage, alcoholic wine was used as an

[14] Moi University Course Notes, PS 2843 "Bible-Wines," Course Hero, accessed August 22, 2017, https://www.coursehero.com/file/p3p88f6/The-art-of-distillation-was-then-unknown-it-was-not-discovered-till-the-ninth/.

[15] Monica Reinagel, "Myths about Sulfites and Wine," Scientific American, July 15, 2017, accessed May 28, 2018, https://www.scientificamerican.com/article/myths-about-sulfites-and-wine/.

[16] Cato the Elder, *De Agri Cultura*, translated and published in the Loeb Classical Library, 1934, http://penelope.uchicago.edu/Thayer/E/Roman/Texts/Cato/De_Agricultura/G*.html.

[17] Ibid, 126-134.

ingredient for making "laxative wine," a "remedy for gout," and a medicine for "retaining urine," but when it came to preparing and preserving grape juice as a beverage, it appears that "sweet wine" was the favorite in Cato's day.[18]

Inspissation, through boiling, was a fourth common means of keeping sweet, unfermented grape juice for years.[19] This method was widely used in Bible times and is still used today.[20] Inspissation is the most relevant form of preservation for this Bible study.[21] Apparent examples of inspissation are seen in Scripture. The respected Jewish Mishna, in the Talmud, refers to "boiled wine,"[22] and such unfermented wine was preferred above alcoholic wine by many secular wine connoisseurs of the biblical era. Inspissation was done by boiling the juice of grapes for several hours. This process not only killed all of the bacteria within the must (preventing fermentation), but also caused all of the ethanol and nearly all of the water to evaporate leaving a concentrated syrupy or condensed, grape paste. Weeks, months, or years later water could be mingled with this condensed, grape honey and a sweet, refreshing nonalcoholic wine was ready for drinking.[23] This same process is used today

---

[18] Ibid.

[19] Farlex Partner Medical Dictionary, "inspissation," The Free Dictionary, accessed August 22, 2017, http://medical-dictionary. thefreedictionary.com/inspissation.

[20] Aromi, "Guerzoni - Mosto Di Uva," Aromiwineandfood.com. accessed August 22, 2017, https://aromiwineandfood.com/product/ guerzoni-mosto-di-uva--grape-must.

[21] William Patton, *Bible Wines* (New York: National Temperance Society, 1874), 26-33.

[22] Joshua Kulp, " Terumot, Chapter Two, Mishnah Six," SHIURIM, accessed August 22, 2017, http://learn.conservativeyeshiva.org/ terumot-chapter-two-mishnah-six/.

[23] Homer, in his famous *Odyssey*, describes a wine preserved in jars for apparently years. This wine was so thick and potent that Homer mixed it with twenty parts water before drinking it. Even after this reconstitution, the wine was so fragrant and delicious that Homer describes it as drink fit for the gods.

to make maple syrup from the clear sap of maple trees. It takes the boiling (inspissation) of forty liters of maple tree sap to make one liter of maple syrup.

William Patton cites seven prominent, secular personalities of the biblical era who refer to *wine* that had undergone inspissation through boiling.[24] Aristotle (384-322 B.C.) said, "The wine of Arcadia [a region of Greece] was so thick that it was necessary to scrape it from the skin bottles in which it was contained, and to dissolve the scrapings in water." Collumella (4-70 A.D.) claimed it was common for the Greeks to "boil their wines." The great wine aficionado, Pliny the Elder (23-79 A.D.), claimed that he had witnessed condensed wine that was several years old and was "the consistency of honey." Horace (65-8 B.C.) testified, "there is no wine sweeter to drink . . . it was like nectar, and more resembled ambrosia than wine; that it was perfectly harmless, and would not produce intoxication."[25] Finally, one of Virgil's (70-19 B.C.) poems describes how "boiled must" produces the most "luscious" or "sweet" wine.[26] It is significant to note that all of these quotes date to the biblical era. **Claiming that people in Bible times did not have means of keeping and preserving nonalcoholic wine is not supported by the facts.** The genuine historical evidence proves that nonalcoholic wine or grape juice was available and often preferred by people of both the Old and New Testaments.

The quotes above are all taken from secular historians, but the Bible also mentions some incidents that I believe are examples of concentrated, nonalcoholic wine by boiling. In 1 Samuel 25:18, "Abigail made haste, and took two hundred loaves, and

---

[24] Homer (c. 1200 - 800 B.C.), Democritus (c. 460-361 B.C.), Aristotle (384-322 B.C.), Virgil (70-19 B.C.), Horace (65-8 B.C.), Collumella (4-70 A.D.), and Pliny (23-79 A.D.).

[25] In ancient Greek mythology, ambrosia was the food of the gods.

[26] William Patton, *Bible Wines*, 41-41.

two bottles of wine, and five sheep ready dressed, and five measures of parched corn, and an hundred clusters of raisins, and two hundred cakes of figs, and laid them on asses." This appears to be food and drink for David and two hundred men. Why did Abigail only give them two bottles of wine? If this wine was fermented, alcoholic liquid wine, as one-wine theory holders claim, it could have only provided drink for a fraction of the men even if the wine was diluted with two or three parts water. However, if this wine was the condensed, powerfully concentrated wine paste described by the historians and poets above, then this sweet, nonalcoholic honey-like wine could have been reconstituted with twenty parts water and could have easily provided sweet drink for two hundred thirsty men.

A second biblical example that supports the assertion that condensed, nonalcoholic wine was available and used by Bible characters is found in 2 Samuel 16:1. David was fleeing Jerusalem to avoid a confrontation with Absalom. "And when David was a little past the top of the hill, behold, Ziba the servant of Mephibosheth met him, with a couple of asses saddled, and upon them two hundred loaves of bread, and an hundred bunches of raisins, and an hundred of summer fruits, and a bottle of wine." Why did Ziba give all these provisions with only "one bottle of wine?" Ziba answers this question in the following verse. "And Ziba said, The asses be for the king's household to ride on; and the bread and summer fruit for the young men to eat; and the wine, that such as be faint in the wilderness may drink" (1 Samuel 16:2).

Most everyone knows that drinking alcohol makes the consumer drowsy. The U.S. Department of Health and Human Services plainly states that, "Drinking alcohol leads to a loss of coordination, poor judgment, slowed reflexes, distorted vision, memory lapses, and even blackouts. This means alcohol won't let you do the things you normally do that require coordination and skill. You can't ride a bike, inline skate, play sports, or even walk in a straight line."[27] Ziba and David were not fools. They knew that alcoholic wine would not energize the "faint." One of the first thing experts recommend for someone who is conscious but feeling faint is "fruit juice."[28] Rather than alcoholic wine, a reasonable conclusion is that Ziba's wine was a preserved bottle of that thick, nonalcoholic wine. David could have mixed the wine with water along the way (2 Samuel 17:21), and it could have refreshed and energized scores of people who were feeling faint during the strenuous journey.

The historical evidence is overwhelming. There were at least four methods of preserving nonalcoholic wine utilized in Bible times. Secular historians and biblical examples are readily available to anyone who is not bound by preconceived, one-wine notions. The historical evidence supports the two-wine position. There were both alcoholic and nonalcoholic wines in the Bible according to historical evidence.

[27] WebMD, "The Buzz about Grape Juice," WebMD.com, accessed August 22, 2017, http://www.webmd.com/food-recipes/features/buzz-about-grape-juice#1.

[28] WebMD, "Fainting Treatment," Webmd.com, accessed August 22, 2017, http://www.webmd.com/first-aid/fainting-treatment.

Grammatical Evidence

This booklet has already asserted that, prior to the twentieth century, the word wine referred to simply the juice of the grape. The Hebrew word *yayin* in the Old Testament (141 appearances) and the Greek word *oinos* in the New Testament (33 appearances) are the most commonly translated words for wine in the Bible. Ferrar Fenton was a master linguist and scholar of the last century. He is said to have known twenty-five languages and translated the entire Bible into English from the original languages. He wrote,

> Wine . . . [referring to both *yayin* and *oinos*] was not confined to an intoxicating liquor made from fruits by alcoholic fermentation of their expressed juices, but more frequently referred to a thick, non-intoxicating Syrup, Conserve, or Jam, produced by boiling, to make them storable as articles of food, exactly as we do at the present day. The only difference being that we store them in jars, bottles, or metal cans, whilst the Ancients laid them up in skin bottles, as Aristotle and Pliny, and other classic writers upon agricultural and household affairs describe. Consequently the contention of some of my correspondents that the Greek *oinos*, *always* meant fermented and intoxicating liquor is totally inaccurate, and only arises from ignorance, or prejudice . . ." [29]

The Jewish Encyclopedia of 1906 defined wine as "the juice of the grape." The article goes on to identify at least a dozen distinct types of wine in the Old

---

[29] Frank Hamilton, *Extracts by Frank Hamilton from The Bible Wine by the late Ferrar Fenton* (London, England: A. & C. Black, Ltd. 1938), 303-304.

Testament - both alcoholic and nonalcoholic wines.[30] *Smith's Bible Dictionary* states, "The simple wines of antiquity were incomparably less deadly than the stupefying and ardent beverages of our western nations. The wines of antiquity were more like sirups [*sic*]; many of them were not intoxicant . . ."[31]

Critics will notice that most of the encyclopedias and dictionaries used to define wine in this book are intentionally older or Jewish. The reason for this is because many modern, western dictionaries have evolved to reflect the contemporary definitions of words like wine and liquor. Sadly, many modern (late 20th century to present) Bible lexicons and dictionaries have also evolved and have changed the original meanings of ancient words to reflect modern words and opinions. This is unfortunate because **the definition of inspired words of Scripture do not evolve or change!** The words of Scripture meant something two or three thousand years ago, and they mean the same thing today. It is as if some people claiming that the Christian temperance movement is a modern phenomenon have created their own counter temperance movement. They produce dictionaries with modern definitions for wine, and then they quote one another in their books and articles while making claims like "all modern scholarship agrees." Every one-wine theory proponent that I can find cites lexicons and dictionaries only produced in the last fifty or sixty years.

The word *wine* was used for both nonalcoholic and alcoholic wine in Hebrew, Greek, Latin, and English prior to the 20th century. This is a grammatical fact. If just one clear case of nonalcoholic wine can be found

---

[30] Emil G. Hirsch and Judah David Eisenstein, "Wine," JewishEncyclopedia.com, accessed August 22, 2017, http://jewishencyclopedia.com/articles/14941-wine.

[31] Cannon Farrar, "Wine," in *Smith's Bible Dictionary*, ed. William Smith (Grand rapids, MI: A.J. Holman, 1884), 1116-1117.

in the Bible, then the grammatical evidence would side with the two-wine position and would completely discredit the one-wine theory. There is not just one clear reference of nonalcoholic wine in the Bible; there are several in both the Old Testament and the New Testament. The following Old Testament examples suffice to prove the point.

Deuteronomy 11:14 and 2 Chronicles 31:5 make similar statements. "That I will give you the rain of your land in his due season, the first rain and the latter rain, that thou mayest gather in thy corn, and thy wine, and thine oil." "And as soon as the commandment came abroad, the children of Israel brought in abundance the firstfruits of corn, wine, and oil, and honey, and of all the increase of the fields; and the tithe of all things brought they in abundantly." In both of these verses, *wine* is being "gathered" and "brought in" from the field. How can grapes freshly harvested from the vineyard be fermented and alcoholic? These are clear examples of wine referring to unfermented grapes or unfermented wine (fresh grape juice).

Nehemiah 13:15 is another irrefutable example. "In those days saw I in Judah some treading wine presses on the sabbath, and bringing in sheaves, and lading asses; as also wine, grapes, and figs, and all manner of burdens, which they brought into Jerusalem on the sabbath day." Nehemiah saw these Sabbath breakers harvesting, pressing, and bringing their freshly pressed grape juice into Jerusalem. The presses were called "wine presses," and the freshly pressed juice was called "wine," but the wine in both cases can only be understood as fresh, unfermented, nonalcoholic wine.

Proverbs 3:9-10 promises a blessing to those who honor the Lord with their "substance." Solomon writes, "thy presses shall burst out with new wine." Once again, freshly pressed grape juice is referred to as *wine*. This cannot be alcoholic wine. This is another solid proof for the two-wine position, and reminds the reader that when God refers to wine that is a blessing, He is referring to new, *nonalcoholic* wine, and not alcoholic wine as the one-wine supporters claim (see also Isaiah 16:10).

A final, indisputable verse is Isaiah 65:8. Jehovah states, "As the new wine is found in the cluster, and one saith, Destroy it not; for a blessing is in it: so will I do for my servants' sakes, that I may not destroy them all." This verse goes so far as to call the liquid or juice, still inside the grape cluster, *wine*! Also, this clearly nonalcoholic wine is once again associated with God's blessing.

Like the historical evidence, the grammatical evidence is overwhelming. Prior to the twentieth century, all the way back through Bible times, the word *wine* referred to the liquid or juice of the grape and could be either alcoholic or nonalcoholic wine. Several scriptural examples of freshly-pressed, nonalcoholic wine have been cited. The grammatical evidence definitively supports the two-wine position.

Theological Evidence

Jehovah said that the *new wine* found in grapes should not be destroyed. Why? "For a blessing is in it" (Isaiah 65:8). Jehovah taught in Deuteronomy 32:33 that the wine of the enemies of God is "poison" and "cruel venom." Psalm 104:15 and Judges 9:13 teach that the wine of the vine cheers the heart of both God and man.[32] While in the same Bible, Proverbs 20:1

---

[32] Some moderate drinkers have argued that phrases like "cheers the heart" or "makes the heart marry" supports the idea that only alcoholic wine could cheer a man's heart. However, the Hebrew word "cheer" in these passages is found 140 times in the Old Testament and the vast majority of the time it has nothing to do with wine. It is simply a word that means joyful or happy and is not a euphemism for getting buzzed or drunk.

warns that, "Wine is a mocker, strong drink is raging: and whosoever is deceived thereby is not wise." Some have tried to argue that Proverbs 20:1 is only a caution against drunkenness. However, this is not an accurate interpretation. In fact, the verse says nothing about drunkenness. The Bible does not say that wine mocks people who get drunk. It does not say that only people who get drunk are deceived. It says that wine *is* a mocker. Alcoholic wine is intrinsically a mocker. Alcoholic wine *is* raging in its very essence. Anyone who argues against these characteristics of alcohol is deceived and unwise.

These descriptions of wine are significant and relate to one's theological understanding of God the Father, God the Son, and God the Holy Spirit. How can an immutable Father say that wine is a "blessing" and "cheers" His heart, and then say that wine is "a mocker," "raging," "poison," and "venom?" How could the Holy Spirit, Who inspired the epistle to the Philippians, tell Timothy to abstain from wine, and then later in the same letter tell him to drink a little wine? How could God command His people not to look at wine (Proverbs 23:31), and then also encourage His people to drink and cheer their hearts with wine? One-wine supporters claim that Jesus broke unfermented bread, but passed fermented wine at the Passover. Either God has Dissociative Identity Disorder and cannot make up His mind about wine, or there are at least two kinds of wine in the Bible. The simple solution to the man-made, one-wine contradiction in the Bible is to understand that there are both alcoholic and nonalcoholic wines in the Bible.

One-wine promoter, Randy Jaeggli, claims that, "There is an apparent paradox in how drinking is presented in the Bible. Scripture sometimes states that wine is a blessing (e.g., Ps. 104:15) and other times calls it a horrible curse (e.g., Prov. 23:29-35)."[33] This "apparent paradox" is only a problem for one-wine holders like Jaeggli. Two-wine proponents see no paradox or contradiction at all. Jaeggli recognizes that "historically" the two-wine position has distinguished the blessed wine as nonalcoholic grape juice and the cursed wine as alcoholic, but he asserts that this is not his personal conclusion.

The Bible teaches that everything God created was "very good" (Genesis 1:31). Even the wine, which Jesus made from water, in John chapter two, was described by the ruler of the feast as "good wine" (John 2:10). However, alcoholic wine contains ethanol. Ethanol is the toxic, flammable, volatile, waste or byproduct of microorganisms that have consumed the sugar in grape juice. Ethanol may be "good" as a paint or varnish solvent, a fuel for a car, or as a disinfectant for killing germs, but ethanol is not *good* for human consumption.[34] The Bible compares alcoholic wine to "poison" and "venom" (Deuteronomy 32:33). Alcohol, poison, and venom are simply not good drinks for people.

I believe that the one-wine theory contradicts the good nature of God and His creation. Like the historical, and grammatical evidence, the theological evidence supports the two-wine theory, much better than the one-wine "paradox."

A final theological allegation can be read on nearly every Christian blog dedicated to the support of the moderate drinking of alcohol. The popular argument goes like this. "Wine is a gift from God for His children to enjoy." This is theological rubbish. God does not create things fermented or brewed. These processes

[33] Randy Jaeggli, *Christians and Alcohol: A Scriptural Case for Abstinence* (Greenville, SC: Bob Jones University Press, 2014), Kindle Location 241.

[34] ChemicalSafetyFacts.org, "Ethanol," accessed May 28, 2018, https://www.chemicalsafetyfacts.org/ethanol/.

are guided by the art and craft of men's hands. The secular wine historian and expert, Paul Lukacs, puts it this way. "No history of wine as we know it can start with its spontaneous fermentation in some unsettled wilderness. Instead, it has to begin when human beings first interfered with nature."[35] God created grapes. The juice of grapes is a gift from God. The humanly manipulated and manufactured products of fermented wine and beer are not gifts from God. They are perversions of God's gift, like adultery and gluttony are perversions of God's gifts of marriage and food.

Medical Evidence

Followers of the one-wine theory often argue that fresh water was often scarce in ancient times and so people would regularly mingle a little wine in their contaminated water to make it potable. There are two huge problems with this argument. First, potable water was not as scarce in biblical times as some have argued. Natural springs, rivers, lakes, and incredible Roman aqueducts were readily available in the first century. People may not have fully understood the concepts of germs and amebas in that day, but the practice of boiling, straining, and treating potentially dangerous water was well known all the way back to the ancient Egyptians.[36]

[35] Paul Lukacs, *Inventing Wine: A New History Of One Of The World's Most Ancient Pleasures* (New York: W. W. Norton & Company, Inc. 2012), 2.

[36] United States Environmental Protection Agency, "The History of Drinking Water Treatment," EPA, accessed May 28, 2018, http://esa21. kennesaw.edu/modules/water/drink-water-trt/drink-water-trt-hist-epa.pdf.

Second, adding a little wine to water does not make it potable. This unscientific argument is frequently used by well meaning, Bible believing scholars and pastors. I have spent days searching in vain for reputable evidence indicating that people prior to the Dark Ages mingled wine with their water for the purpose of making it safe to drink. Searching for modern, verifiable evidence that wine or alcohol even has the capability of treating potentially dangerous water in order to make it safe to drink is also futile. This false narrative can be found written and taught throughout Christian circles, but absolutely no original documentation or citation is ever offered. It is simply assumed because Dr. Big Name said it or wrote it.

The National Center for Biotechnology Information has actually studied the survival of bacterial enteropathogens in alcoholic drinks. They put four harmful intestinal bacteria into water and froze this water into ice cubes. The ice cubes were then deposited in multiple alcoholic drinks. The three scientists reported that, "none of the organisms were completely eliminated as a result of freezing for 24 hours followed by melting in any of the test drinks, even when the drink was 86-proof tequila."[37]

Richard Teachout is the author of *Grape Juice in the Bible: God's Blessing for His People!* Teachout asked an expert at the Safe Drinking Water Foundation in Canada, "What percentage of alcohol would have to be added to make unsafe water safe?"

---

[37] D. L. Dickens, H. L. DuPont, and P. C. Johnson, "Survival of bacterial enteropathogens in the ice of popular drinks," National Center for Biotechnology Information, accessed August 22, 2017, https://www.ncbi.nlm.nih.gov/pubmed/3889393. "86-proof tequila" refers to an alcoholic drink that is 43% alcohol. In the Unites States alcohol proof refers to twice the percentage of alcohol by volume in a drink. Therefore, 100-proof whisky contains 50% alcohol by volume.

The authority laughed and said, "100%!"[38] The notion that ancients added one or two parts alcoholic wine (normally 5% or less alcohol in Bible times) to water in order to make it safe to drink is absurd and unscientific. This is apparently a counter temperance wives' tale that cannot be substantiated by historical documentation or modern expert verification, but continues to be propagated in many churches and seminaries.

One medical benefit of nonalcoholic wine was already pointed out from the text in 2 Samuel 16:1 (fruit juice can revive the faint). A second medical benefit of nonalcoholic wine will be established later when 1 Timothy 5:23 is examined in detail.

The only condoned medicinal use for *alcoholic* wine in the Bible was as an anesthetic before death.[39] The anesthetic before death was not really a refreshing beverage, but rather a strong, numbing medicine. This type of drink was called a "strong drink" in Proverbs 31:6, "Give strong drink unto him that is ready to perish . . ." and "vinegar" in

[38] Richard Teachout, *Grape Juice in the Bible: God's Blessing for His People!* (Quebec Canada: Etude Biblique pour Aujourd'hui, 2011), 78.

[39] It appears that the good Samaritan used "wine" as an antiseptic in Luke 10:34. However, wine is not actually an effective antiseptic. Hippocrates, the "Father of Medicine," taught that wine could be used medicinally - including as an antiseptic. Jancis Robinson, *The Oxford Companion to Wine,* 3rd ed. (Oxford University Press, 2006), 433. For centuries, people believed Hippocrates' incorrect theory. It is known today that an effective alcoholic antiseptic must be 60-90% alcohol. Alcoholic wine in Bible times typically contained around 5% alcohol and could not possibly exceed 20% because distillation of alcohol was not yet practiced. In the words of Dr. Christine Princeton, the disinfecting ability of a solution under 35% alcohol is "practically nil" (http://disaster medicine-christine.blogspot.com/2010/03/to-booze-or-not-to-booze-alcohol-as.html).

Matthew 27:33-34, "And when they were come unto a place called Golgotha, that is to say, a place of a skull, They gave [Jesus] vinegar to drink mingled with gall: and when he had tasted thereof, **he would not drink**.". Jesus rejected this type of alcoholic drink (Mark 15:23), and so should you.

It is interesting to note that the immediate context of Proverbs 31 forbids kings and their children from drinking "wine" or "strong drink." Priests were also forbidden from drinking "wine" and "strong drink" when serving the Lord (Leviticus 10:9). In the New Testament, the children of God are made kings and priests when Jesus washes them with His blood (Revelation 1:6). Therefore, **all New Testament saints are kings and priests in God's eyes.** I believe that New Testament Christian kings and priests should not drink alcoholic wine for the same reasons offered in Proverbs 31 and Leviticus 10.

Nonalcoholic wine can revive a fainting person, and treat certain minor infirmities. Alcoholic wine was suggested in the Bible as a deathbed anesthetic. However, it was taboo for kings and priests and was rejected by Jesus during His crucifixion (Mark 15:23).

So, what is wine? **Wine is a general term for liquid or juice of the grape.** Are there different kinds of wine in the Bible? The historical, grammatical, theological, and medical evidence is overwhelming. There were *both* alcoholic and nonalcoholic wines mentioned throughout Scripture. Only the context can reveal the distinction, not the term itself. God's Word teaches that nonalcoholic wine is a blessing (Isaiah 65:8; Judges 9:13), and alcoholic wine is a curse (Proverbs 21:1; 23:29-35).

Three Misunderstood Scripture Passages Referring To Wine

A solid understanding of the previous material should help clarify many confusing and controversial Bible passages. This booklet will examine three of the most misinterpreted and misunderstood Scripture narratives about wine.

Did Jesus Make Alcoholic Wine?

In the second chapter of John, the beloved disciple describes the first miracle of Jesus' earthly ministry. Jesus, Mary, and the disciples were invited to a wedding in Cana. The hosts ran out of wine. Jesus took six large pots of water and miraculously transformed the water into wine. Having established that wine in the Bible is simply juice of the grape, the real question is "Did Jesus make alcoholic wine or nonalcoholic wine (grape juice)?"

The nature of Christ supports the position that this wine was grape juice. Patton asks,

> Is it not derogatory to the character of Christ and the teachings of the Bible to suppose that He exerted his miraculous power to produce . . . wine which inspiration had denounced as "a mocker," as "biting like a serpent," and "stinging like an adder," as "the poison of dragons," "the cruel venom of asps," and which the Holy Ghost had selected as the emblem of the wrath of God Almighty? Is it probable that He gave that to the guests?[40]

The rhetorical answer to Patton's final question is "No way." It is, rather, more in line with the nature and

---

[40] Patton, *Bible Wines*, 89-90.

character of God to have created and offered "new wine" that contains a blessing (Isaiah 65:8). Since any creative act of a thrice holy God is "good" (perfect in essence - totally absent of any degradation), it would be a violation of His character to create anything that was already degraded. Creating nonalcoholic grape juice is much more characteristic of the nature of God.

The nature of creation and miracles supports the position that this wine was grape juice. Does God not already "miraculously" produce this same unfermented, nonalcoholic juice of the grape every season in the vine cluster of the branch (Psalm 104:14-15)? Creating something fermented would have been a break from His annual habit of transforming the water of the earth into the juice He creates in every grape of every vine in the world.[41] Creating fermented wine would have been uncharacteristically different than any of His other creations or miracles.

The description of the wine supports the position that this wine was grape juice. The ruler of the feast specifically described the wine that Jesus made as "good wine". Once again, the Bible describes new wine as a blessing, but alcoholic wine is always warned against or presented in a negative light. The fact that the ruler of the feast described it as "good wine" better supports the position that the wine, which Jesus made, was sweet grape juice. This grape juice was possibly the sweetest, most delicious, most fragrant wine mankind had ever tasted.

The quantity of the wine supports the position that this wine was grape juice. Drunkenness is always condemned in Scripture and was unacceptable behavior in both the religious and secular first-century crowds. One firkin was about 36 liters. Jesus, therefore, made between 432 and 648 liters of wine

---

[41] Richard Chenevix Trench, *Miracles of Our Lord* (London: D. Appleton and Company, 1846), 105.

(2:6)! According to the ruler's speech in verse ten, the people at the wedding had already had plenty to drink. Offering nearly five hundred liters of alcoholic wine to people who had already had quite a bit to drink would have only encouraged and promoted drunkenness. I absolutely do not accept the suggestion that Jesus turned water into alcoholic wine. The nature of Christ, the nature of creation, the description of the wine, and the amount of wine created all support the opinion that this wine was sweet, unfermented, un-intoxicating, "good wine," or grape juice.

Did Jesus Command Christians To Drink Alcoholic Wine?

All three of the synoptic Gospels describe the Passover meal Jesus shared with his disciples. Some one-wine opinion holders will argue that since Jesus gave wine to his disciples during this meal, and since all wine in the Bible contained alcohol, it must be acceptable for Christians to drink alcohol in moderation. This syllogism is erroneous in all three points. First, the Bible does not even say that Jesus drank or offered "wine" to his disciples during the Last

Supper. Second, this booklet has proven beyond doubt that freshly pressed grape juice is found in several places in the Bible and that nonalcoholic wine was common in Bible times. Therefore, the conclusion that moderate drinking of alcohol is acceptable because Jesus did it is also a false assumption. The Bible never states that Jesus drank alcohol.

Many people wrongly assume that the drink of the Last Supper was fermented wine. The *Code of Canon Law* and the *Catechism of the Catholic Church* require Roman Catholics to drink only fermented, grape-wine in their celebration of the Eucharist.[42] They assume that fermented wine is what Jesus gave to His disciples. But what do the Scriptures actually say? **All three synoptic Gospels refer to the drink of communion as "fruit of the vine"** (Matthew 26:29; Mark 14:25; Luke 22:18). Even Paul's instructions concerning the Lord's Supper in 1 Corinthians 11:17-34 harshly condemn drunkenness and refer to the second element of communion only as "the cup of the

---

[42] Vatican, "Chapter III: The Proper Celebration Of Mass," Congregation for Divine Worship and the Discipline of the Sacrament, accessed August 22, 2017, http://www.vatican.va/roman_curia/congregations/ccdds/documents/rc_con_ccdds_doc_20040423_redemptionis-sacramentum_en.html#Chapter III.

Lord" (11:27). The word *wine* is completely absent from all of the accounts and teaching about the Lord's Supper! Jesus refers to the drink as the fruit or product of the grape vine. As wine expert, Lukacs, pointed out earlier, fermented grape wine is an "interference" of nature or a product of man. Fresh, unfermented grape juice is a product of the vine or actually a product of the Lord's making.

The Scriptures avoid the term *wine* in all of the communion passages. Not only is the clearer phrase "fruit of the vine" used, but God's Word and Hebrew tradition also forbid fermentation during the Passover week. God's command to His people in Exodus 12:15 is unmistakable and severe. "Seven days shall ye eat unleavened bread; even the first day ye shall put away leaven out of your houses: for whosoever eateth leavened bread from the first day until the seventh day, that soul shall be cut off from Israel." All leaven was to be removed from their homes during the Passover week. The consequence for disobedience was eternal! Some form of leaven is required to ferment wine. **Drinking fermented wine during the Passover week would have been a direct violation of God's command in Exodus.** Jesus never violated God's laws or commandments (Matthew 5:17). Therefore, both the bread and the grape juice offered by Christ in the communion was unfermented and in compliance to God's commands given in Exodus chapter twelve.

Did Paul Instruct Timothy to Drink Alcoholic Wine?

In the first epistle of the Apostle Paul to Pastor Timothy, one can find a number of references to wine. It has already been established that wine is a general term for the liquid or juice of the grape, and that only the context can determine if the wine is alcoholic or nonalcoholic. Therefore, it is essential to study previous references to wine in 1 Timothy before directly addressing Paul's instruction to his son in the faith in 1 Timothy 5:23.

In 1 Timothy chapter three, Paul delineates the necessary qualifications of a bishop, a deacon, and his wife. Among those standards is the requirement that the pastor be, "not given to wine" (1 Timothy 3:3). The English phrase "given to wine" comes from a compound word in Greek, *pároinon*. This compound word is made up of the two, Greek root words, *pár* and *oinos*. The Greek word *pár* literally means "by" or "over," and the Greek word *oinos* has already been translated "wine" and defined as "the liquid or juice of the grape." The literal standard here then is that Pastors must be people "not by wine." The famous commentator, Albert Barnes, explains:

> The Greek word (*paroinos*) occurs in the New Testament only here [1 Tim 3:3] and in Titus 1:7. It means, properly, *by wine*; that is, spoken of what takes place *by* or *over* wine . . . Then it denotes, as it does here, one who sits by wine; that is, who is in the habit of drinking it . . . It means that one who is in the *habit* of drinking wine, or who is accustomed to sit with those who indulge in it, should not be admitted to the ministry. The way in which the apostle mentions the subject here would lead us fairly to suppose that he did not mean to commend its use in any sense; that he regarded it as dangerous and that he would wish the ministers of religion to avoid it altogether.[43]

There is little doubt or debate that Paul is referring to alcoholic wine in this instance. How could he be referring to all wine or to nonalcoholic wine when

---

[43] Albert Barnes, *Notes, Explanatory and Practical on the Epistles of Paul to the Thessalonians, to Timothy, to Titus and to Philemon* (New York: Harper & Brothers Publishers, 1873), 140.

Jesus commanded His disciples to remember Him "as oft as ye drink" the "fruit of the vine" each communion service (1 Corinthians 11:25)? This is a difficult contradiction for one-wine proponents, but when one understands that Jesus mandates unfermented wine in the Lord's Supper, and forbids His ministers to be near fermented wine, there is no confusion.

Being confident that Paul instructs Timothy and other church leaders to be men who abstain from both the presence and consumption of alcoholic wine, one may then turn to chapter five of the same letter. In 1 Timothy 5:23, Paul wrote, "Drink no longer water, but use a little wine for thy stomach's sake and thine often infirmities." If one holds the one-wine theory position, then an explanation must be given to avoid a contradiction between chapters three and five. The most common explanation is that Paul is making an exception to the normal pastoral abstinence standard exclusively to Timothy for medicinal purposes.

There are two common suggestions offered to support this theory. Some suggest that Timothy did not have easy access to good clean potable water and, therefore, Paul was suggesting that he add a little alcoholic wine to his water to make it drinkable. This untenable idea was debunked earlier when the "Medical Evidence" was examined. The second common suggestion is that Timothy may have had gastritis or a stomach ulcer.[44] If this were true, Paul would have never suggested adding alcohol to his drinking water. The first recommendation of doctors to patients with ulcers is to stop smoking and drinking alcohol.[45] Alcohol is about the worst thing a person can drink if he has stomach problems. The U.K. based

[44] John MacArthur, *The Superiority of Christ* (Chicago, IL: Moody Press, 1986), 137.
[45] WebMD, "What Is Peptic Ulcer Disease?" WebMD.com, accessed August 22, 2017, http://www.webmd.com/digestive-disorders/digestive-diseases-peptic-ulcer-disease#1.

charity, Drinkaware, warns, "Put simply, alcohol irritates your digestive system. Drinking – even a little – makes your stomach produce more acid than usual, which can in turn cause gastritis (the inflammation of the stomach lining). This triggers stomach pain, vomiting, diarrhoea and, in heavy drinkers, even bleeding."[46]

The fact that Paul, via inspiration, told Timothy to drink a little wine for his "stomach's sake" is a powerful support for the proposition that the wine he was suggesting in chapter five was nonalcoholic, grape juice wine. This would eliminate any perceived contradiction to the mandate in chapter three and makes much more sense. Medical advice for people with stomach ulcers, urinary tract infections and/or acid reflux all include the recommendations to drink, "low-acid fruit juices such as apple juice and grape juice. Drink plenty of water, and avoid alcoholic beverages."[47] Is it not reasonable to assume that the omniscient Holy Spirit would give the same advice to Timothy for his stomach problems?

Suggesting that Paul was forbidding alcoholic wine in 1 Timothy 3:3 and then recommending alcoholic wine in 1 Timothy 5:23 would be a contradiction of Scripture (in the immediate context), a contradiction of sound logic, and a contradiction of popular, proven medical science. A sound conclusion then is that Paul was reinforcing God's Old Testament mandate of abstinence for his ministers and leaders in chapter

---

[46] Drinkaware, "Is Alcohol Harming Your Stomach?" Drinkaware.com, accessed August 22, 2017, https://www.drinkaware.co.uk/alcohol-facts/health-effects-of-alcohol/effects-on-the-body/is-alcohol-harming-your-stomach/.

[47] Robin Doyle, "What Can I Eat & Drink with a Peptic Ulcer?" Livestrong.com, accessed August 22, 2017, http://www.livestrong.com/article/340876-what-can-i-eat-drink-with-a-peptic-ulcer/.

three,[48] and later in the same letter, he was recommending that Timothy add a little low-acid fruit juice to his water for his stomach's sake.

As a side note, some supporters of moderate drinking have tried to argue that 1 Timothy 3:8 implies that drinking a "little" alcohol is fine as long as you don't get drunk. Paul was listing the qualifications for deacons in this verse when he wrote, "Likewise must the deacons be grave, not doubletongued, not given to much wine, not greedy of filthy lucre." The argument claims that deacons and Christians in general should not drink "much wine" but that a little wine is acceptable. This is bad reasoning. Just because much of something is expressly forbidden does not prove or imply that little of that thing is permissible. For example, Solomon commands his audience to avoid "much wickedness" in Ecclesiastes 7:17. Nobody takes this command and argues that "much wickedness" is bad, but a little wickedness is fine.

The key to understanding 1 Timothy 3:8 is the English word "given" (*proséchontas* in Greek). This word has the idea of being mentally obsessed, captivated, or addicted to something. In truth, **Christians should not be "given" to anything temporal!** They should not be given to much wine, little wine, coffee, Coca Cola, or anything else. Paul used this exact same word in Titus 1:14. He wrote, "Not giving heed [*proséchontas*] to Jewish fables . . ." It would be ridiculous to argue from this passage that giving heed to Jewish fables or lies is bad, but giving heed to Greek fables and lies is acceptable. It is just as inconsistent and invalid to argue that 1 Timothy 3:8 somehow approves the moderate drinking of alcohol.

To argue that God forbids "given to much wine" but allows given to *little* wine from 1 Timothy 3:8 is as

---

[48] God demanded total abstinence of kings and priests in the Old Testament, and I believe that He expects total abstinence of pastors, deacons, and all other believers (New Testament kings and priests) today.

unreasonable as saying the rest of the verse teaches that greedy of filthy money is bad, but greedy of clean money is fine. No, this is poor logic and bad exegesis. Both "given" to something in moderation and excess is wrong, just as "greedy" of something legal or illegal is wrong.

In summary, a careful examination of John 2:1-11 points to the assertion that Jesus made water into "good," fresh grape juice at the wedding in Cana of Galilee. A consideration of the synoptic accounts of the Passover meal, and Paul's guidelines about the Lord's Supper in 1 Corinthians, teach that "the fruit of the vine" offered in the "Lord's cup" during communion was and should be unfermented grape juice. Finally, the context and the leading medical advice of today support the opinion that Paul was suggesting a little fresh grape juice in 1 Timothy 5:23, rather than alcoholic wine. The next section of this book will provide five biblical principles that demand Christians abstain from alcohol in all of its forms.

Five Biblical Principles Demanding Abstinence From Alcohol

Do Not Fellowship With The Unfruitful Works Of Darkness

Ephesians 5:11 requires, "And have no fellowship with the unfruitful works of darkness, but rather reprove them." The very first and prime example of an unfruitful work of darkness in the context of this commandment is, "And be not drunk with wine, wherein is excess . . ." (Ephesians 5:18). Without question, drunkenness is a sin and an unfruitful work of darkness. However, drinking alcohol is also an unfruitful work of darkness. The Anti-Saloon League of the last century insisted that, "by conservative estimate, 19% of divorces, 25% of poverty, 25% of insanity, 37% of [welfare aid], 45% of child desertion, and 50% of all crime in America were directly attributed to alcohol consumption."[49] These statistics reflect the fruits of drinking alcohol. **Not all of these crimes and costs were caused by *drunkenness*, but all of them were caused by *drinking alcohol.*** The Bible also describes other results of drinking alcohol. Drinking alcohol leads to,

> . . . drunkenness, nakedness (Genesis 9:21), and incest (Genesis 19:32). It is described as the poison of dragons, and the venom of snakes (Deuteronomy 32:33). Alcohol leads to divorce (Esther 1:10). God said it is consumed by the wicked (Psalm 75:8). It leads to violence (Proverbs 4:17), poverty (Proverbs 21:17), woe, sorrow, contentions, babblings, wounds without cause, and redness of eyes (Proverbs 23:29). Alcohol is bitter to them that drink it (Isaiah 24:9). It causes beauty to fade (Isaiah 28:1). It leads people to make errors of vision and errors of judgment, and leads them in the wrong way (Isaiah 28:7). Alcohol is an illustration of the wrath of God (Jeremiah 25:15) It leads to defilement (Daniel 1:8). It can take a man's heart away from God and to prostitutes (Hosea 4:11), and it is an illustration of God's condemnation (Amos 2:8).[50]

These are the results of drinking alcohol. Most Christians agree that they should not get drunk, but the actual mandate is "have no fellowship" with the ungodly practice of drinking alcohol. Fellowship means to share company or to participate with something. A Christian's testimony is normally tarnished, if not

[49] Randy Jaeggli, *Christians and Alcohol*, Kindle Location 1610.
[50] Ben Sinclair, *Spiritual Growth Series* (Bamenda, Cameroon: Gospel Press, 2010), 88.

destroyed in the eyes of unbelievers, when he fellowships and participates in the drinking of alcohol - even in moderation.

Daniel L. Akin correctly asserts that, "Moderation is not the cure for the liquor problem. Moderation is the cause of the liquor problem. Becoming an alcoholic does not begin with the last drink, it always begins with the first. Just leave it alone."[51] Christians should abstain from drinking wine and alcohol because God commanded His children to, "have no fellowship with the unfruitful works of darkness, but rather reprove them."

Make No Room For The Devil

A second biblical principle that demands abstinence from drinking alcohol is found in Ephesians 4:27 which reads, "Neither give place to the devil." This command means that we should not allow Satan any space or room in our lives.

Medical researchers say that within minutes of drinking just one or two glasses of alcoholic wine, the senses are dulled and a person's judgment to make quick and right decisions is clouded. Tests indicate that the person drinking the wine often cannot even feel the alcohol's influences until the third glass. By then, the person is completely under the influence of the alcohol.

Countless people have argued, "I drink some, but not enough to get drunk." This is the statement of a self-deceived person (Proverbs 20:1), who admits to giving Satan *some* room or influence in his life. This person is trying to say, "I allow Satan a little room in my life, but I don't allow him to control my whole life."

---

[51] Daniel L. Akin, "The Emerging Church and Ethical Choices: The Corinthian Matrix," in *Evangelicals Engaging Emergent: A Discussion of the Emergent Church Movement*, ed. William D. Henard and Adam W. Greenway (Nashville, TN: B&H Publishing Group, 2009), 278.

This is foolishness, and contradicts the commands to be *completely* submitted to and *fully* controlled by the Holy Spirit (Ephesians 5:18b). Christians are commanded to, "make *no* provision for the flesh" (Romans 13:14).[52]

Do Not Cause Your Brother To Stumble

A third biblical principle that demands Christians abstain from drinking alcoholic wine, beer or whisky is the stern warning not to offend or to cause a brother to stumble. Romans 14:13 commands, "Let us not therefore judge one another any more: but judge this rather, that no man put a stumblingblock or an occasion to fall in his brother's way." A stumbling block is *anything* that causes someone to trip and fall. The verse is directly addressing brothers in Christ (both Jews and Gentiles). Followers of Christ should never lead their brothers to sin by their example - even if the more mature or informed brother does not believe the activity is sin.

Charles Spurgeon, the famous Baptist preacher of London, smoked cigars and drank wine in his early life and ministry. Just because famous men of God do a particular activity does not make that activity right or moral. People did not know that smoking was dangerous to health in those days, and Spurgeon had not yet learned of unfermented wine.[53] It was the "stumbling block" principle that reportedly led Spurgeon to eventually give up both smoking and drinking.[54] Spurgeon may not have originally believed

---

[52] The emphasis in this verse was made by the writer.

[53] After Spurgeon joined the temperance movement and publically became an abstainer from alcohol, he required that his church use only "Frank Wright's Unfermented Wine" in the communion at the Metropolitan Tabernacle. Charles Spurgeon, *C. H. Spurgeon's Autobiography* (London: Passmore and Alabaster, 1900), 135.

[54] R. Kent Hughes, *Romans: Righteousness From Heaven* (Wheaton, IL: Crossway, 1991), 260-265.

that smoking or drinking were personal sins for him. However, when he was older, and had children of his own, and knew that many people followed his example, he eventually became a strong, public supporter of total abstinence. He announced from his pulpit, "If it will strengthen and encourage a single soul among the 5,000 that are here, I will put [the blue ribbon of abstinence] on."[55] As his conviction for total abstinence intensified, he later wrote, **"Next to the preaching of the Gospel, the most necessary thing to be done in England is to induce our people to become abstainers."**[56] Apparently preaching the Gospel and preaching abstinence were Spurgeon's top two preaching priorities. This is a profound opinion, and reveals how significant, evil, and influential the binding sin of alcoholism is.

Alcohol is a stumbling block to many saved and unsaved people. God's Word commands believers never to be a stumbling block to others. The stumbling block principle alone should be mandate and motivation enough for all Christians to commit to total abstinence. Paul was serious about his commitment to never trip his Jewish brothers. Even though eating meat was not a sin, he was willing to become a vegetarian the rest of his life in order to prevent leading weaker brethren to sin against their consciences (1 Corinthians 8:10-13). Christians today should be willing to make this same commitment of abstinence from alcohol because of their love for others. Christians should never drink alcohol in any form lest they become a stumbling block to their brothers and sisters.

---

[55] Lewis Drummond, *Spurgeon: Prince of Preachers* (Grand Rapids, MI: Kregel Publications,1992), 440.

[56] Ibid, 440.

Treat Your Body As The Temple Of The Holy Ghost

First Corinthians 6:19-20 asks and answers a very important question directed at Christians. "What? know ye not that your body is the temple of the Holy Ghost which is in you, which ye have of God, and ye are not your own? For ye are bought with a price: therefore glorify God in your body, and in your spirit, which are God's." According to this letter to the church in Corinth, Christians should only eat and drink things that glorify God (1 Corinthians 10:31). A Christian should never eat or drink things that knowingly harm or damage their body.

The Holy Spirit dwells in the body of every believer. God calls the body of each believer His temple. He demands that we protect our bodies from defilement of all forms. 1 Corinthians 3:16-17 are even more direct in their insistence and warning. "Know ye not that ye are the temple of God, and that the Spirit of God dwelleth in you? If any man defile the temple of God, him shall God destroy; for the temple of God is holy, which temple ye are." The Bible is clear. Intentionally defiling your body with harmful substances or activities will lead to the destruction of your body at the hand of God.

The authors of "the most comprehensive estimate of the global burden of alcohol use to date" considered 592 studies which included 28 million people from 195 countries.[57] This massive study found that in 2016 alcohol was associated with 2.8 million deaths worldwide.[58] "Among the population aged 15–49 years,

---

[57] Robyn Burton and Nick Sheron, "No Level of Alcohol Consumption Improves Health," *The Lancet*, published online August 23, 2018, accessed August 28, 2018, https://www.thelancet.com/journals/lancet/article/PIIS0140-6736(18)31571-X/fulltext.

[58] Emmanuela Gakidou and Global Burden of Disease 2016 Alcohol Collaborators, "Alcohol Use and Burden for 195 Countries and Territories, 1990–2016: A Systematic Analysis for the Global Burden of Disease Study 2016," *The Lancet*, published online August 23, 2018, accessed August 28, 2018, https://www.thelancet.com/action/showPdf?pii=S0140-6736%2818%2931310-2.

alcohol use was the leading risk factor globally."[59] Sixteen percent of deaths in this same age bracket were attributed to alcohol use.[60]

Previous studies and health reports have suggested that an occasional glass of alcoholic, red wine "may" have some heart health benefits. This new study states that this suggestion remains an open question and is a statistically insignificant proposition. The report concludes by stating, "The widely held view of the health benefits of alcohol needs revising, particularly as improved methods and analyses continue to show how much alcohol use contributes to global death and disability. Our results show that the safest level of drinking is none."[61] The study identified 60 acute and chronic diseases directly linked to alcohol consumption.

A second enormous study on the harm of drinking alcohol was published in 2018.[62] More than 100 scientists and medical doctors tracked the habits of about 600,000 drinkers from 19 different countries. The results of this enormous study led to the following conclusions. People who drink one or more glasses of wine per day are statistically lowering their life expectancy by 2-5 years or more![63] **There are no safe drinking limits.**

---

[59] Ibid.

[60] Ibid. This statistic includes illnesses, road-casualties, and suicides.

[61] Ibid.

[62] Angela M. Wood and about 120 other doctors and scientist, "Risk Thresholds For Alcohol Consumption: Combined Analysis Of Individual-Participant Data For 599,912 Current Drinkers In 83 Prospective Studies," The Lancet, Volume 391, Number 10129: 1455-1548, accessed April 22, 2018, http://www.thelancet.com/journals/lancet/article/PIIS0140-6736(18)30134-X/fulltext.

[63] Alex Matthews-King, "Glass Of Wine A Day Could Shave Years Off Your Life Warns Study Calling For Global Reduction Of Alcoholic Limits," Independent.co.uk, accessed April 21, 2018, https://www.independent.co.uk/news/health/alcohol-death-drinking-life-expectancy-safe-limits-reduced-beer-wine-pint-glass-cambridge-a8301876.html.

Even low level drinking is linked to shorter life expectancies. "Alcohol consumption at any level was associated with higher risk of stroke, heart failure, fatal hypertensive disease (high blood pressure) and fatal aneurysms."[64] Professor Chico of cardiovascular medicine at the University of Sheffield summarized the massive study by simply stating that when all the evidence is considered, "There are no health benefits from drinking alcohol."

Remember, this book has already pointed out what alcohol is. Alcohol is the byproduct or toxic excrement of yeasts and other microorganisms after consuming the sugars in grape juice or some other sugary liquids. **God simply calls alcohol poison** (Deuteronomy 32:33). People who argue that a glass of red wine contains antioxidants often do not realize that these heart healthy antioxidants are not from the alcohol, but rather come from the grapes that produce the wine. Drs. Bertelli and Das assert that "antioxidants, including resveratrol, catechin, epicatechin, and proanthocyanidins" come from the grapes, not the alcohol in wine. They go on to explain that, "Resveratrol is mainly found in the grape skin, whereas proanthocyanidins are found only in the seeds. Recent studies have demonstrated that resveratrol and proanthocyanidin are the major compounds present in grapes and wines responsible for cardioprotection."[65]

The bottom line is this. Grapes and nonalcoholic grape juice have *many* proven health benefits. Alcohol has *zero*, proven, long-term health benefits but *many* proven damaging dangers, risks, and harms. The same is true for alcohol consumed in grape wine, whisky, beer or any other alcoholic drink.

---

[64] Ibid.

[65] A. A. Bertelli and D. K. Das, " Grapes, Wines, Resveratrol, and Heart Health," National Center for Biotechnical Information, accessed April 22, 2018, https://www.ncbi.nlm.nih.gov/pubmed/19770673.

Drinking alcohol affects every part of your body. **Alcohol affects the brain.** Drinking interferes with the brain's communication pathways, and can affect the way the brain looks and works. These disruptions can change mood and behavior, and make it harder to think clearly and move with coordination.   **Alcohol affects the heart.** Drinking can damage the heart, causing problems including: cardiomyopathy (stretching and drooping of heart muscle), arrhythmias (irregular heart beat), stroke, and high blood pressure.

Alcohol affects the liver. Heavy drinking takes a toll on the liver, and can lead to a variety of problems and liver inflammations including: steatosis, alcoholic hepatitis, fibrosis, and cirrhosis.

Alcohol affects the pancreas. Alcohol causes the pancreas to produce toxic substances that can eventually lead to pancreatitis, a dangerous inflammation and swelling of the blood vessels in the pancreas that prevents proper digestion.

Alcohol affects the body's immune system. Drinking can weaken your immune system, making your body a much easier target for disease. Regular drinkers are more liable to contract diseases like pneumonia and tuberculosis than people who do not drink.

Alcohol affects every system, organ and cell in the entire body! Drinking too much alcohol can increase your risk of developing certain cancers, including cancers of the mouth, esophagus, throat, liver, and breast.[66]

The latest, most comprehensive medical research reveals that drinking alcohol will reduce your life

---

[66] These six paragraphs are adapted directly from a publication produced by the U.S. government's National Institute on Alcohol Abuse and Alcoholism. The stated purpose of this organization is, "Understanding the impact of alcohol on human health and well-being." National Institute on Alcohol Abuse and Alcoholism, "Alcohol's Effects on the Body," Niaaa.nih.gov, accessed April 23, 2018, https://www.niaaa.nih.gov/alcohol-health/alcohols-effects-body.

expectancy, and will negatively affect your health on many levels. Christians should never drink alcohol because it shortens their life and damages the temple of the Holy Ghost (the body).

Be Sober

The principles of "Do Not Fellowship With The Unfruitful Works Of Darkness," "Make No Room For The Devil," "Do Not Cause Your Brother To Stumble," and "Treat Your Body As The Temple Of The Holy Ghost" should be more than enough evidence to convince any child of God to be a total abstainer of alcohol drinks in any form. However, if those principles are not enough, this fifth principle is irrefutable. God commands all of His followers to "Be Sober!"

Paul writes to all children of God in 1 Thessalonians 5:5-8 and commands, "Ye are all the children of light, and the children of the day: we are not of the night, nor of darkness. Therefore let us not sleep, as do others; but let us watch and be sober. For they that sleep sleep in the night; and they that be drunken are drunken in the night. But let us, who are of the day, be sober . . ." Notice the stark contrasts made in these verses. There are children of light and day, and there are children of dark and night. There are no children of dawn or dusk. There are those "that be drunken" and those who are "sober." **Just as there is no middle ground between children of light and dark, there is no middle ground between sober and drunk permitted in the Bible.** The Bible does not allow for, "drink but don't get drunk." The Bible does not allow for social or moderate drinking. Twice in this passage, the Bible commands "all the children of light" to "be sober!"

There should be no uncertainty about the meaning of the command to "be sober" (*nepho* in Greek).

Counter temperance advocates may try to use contemporary modern definitions, but reputable, historical references allow for no uncertainty. Strong's Concordance says that "be sober" (in 1 Thessalonians 5:6 and 8) means, "to abstain from wine."[67] Vine's dictionary defines "be sober" as, "to be free from the influence of intoxicants."[68] Samuele Bacchiocchi sites several sources. He writes,

> There is noteworthy unanimity among Greek lexicons on the primary meaning of this verb. Liddell and Scott give as the first meaning of *nepho*, "to be sober, drink no wine." In his *Patristic Greek Lexicon*, Lampe renders it, "be temperate, drink no wine." . . . Donnegan defines *nepho* as "to live abstemiously, to abstain from wine;" Greene, "to be sober, not intoxicated;" Robinson, "to be sober, temperate, abstinent, especially in respect to wine;" Abbott-Smith, "to be sober, abstain from wine."[69]

Nowhere does the Bible allow for social or moderate drinking. Nowhere does the Bible allow for anything between abstinence and drunkenness. A person who drinks one or two glasses of wine may not be drunk, but according to the Scriptures, *he is no longer sober.*

For those who might like to argue that the biblical mandate for total abstinence is mental or spiritual rather than physical, Peter dispels this argument by demanding total abstinence in *both* mind and body in

---

[67] James Strong, "G3525: νήφω nḗphō," Blue Letter Bible, accessed August 22, 2017, https://www.blueletterbible.org/lang/lexicon/lexicon.cfm?Strongs=G3525&t=KJV&ss=1.

[68] William Edwy Vine, "B-1 Verb Strong's Number: G3525," Blue Letter Bible, accessed August 22, 2017, https://www.blueletterbible.org/search/Dictionary/viewTopic.cfm?topic=VT0002682.

[69] Samuele Bacchiocchi, *Wine in the Bible* (Berrien Springs, MI: Biblical Perspectives, 2001), 170-171.

his first epistle. "Wherefore gird up the loins of your mind, be sober, and hope to the end for the grace that is to be brought unto you at the revelation of Jesus Christ" (1 Peter 1:13). "Be sober, be vigilant; because your adversary the devil, as a roaring lion, walketh about, seeking whom he may devour" (1 Peter 5:8). The devil knows he cannot "devour" the eternal souls of believers, so he attacks Christians in their minds and bodies. Christians should abstain from alcoholic wine in order to be perfectly sober in body *and* mind, and to be able, by the grace of God, to resist his subtle but devastating attacks.

Conclusion

The controversy between abstinence and moderate drinking will continue until all believers drink sweet, new grape juice together with Jesus in the eternal kingdom of God (Mark 14:25). In the mean time, There will always be some who drink of "the cup of the Lord," and some who drink of "the cup of devils" (1 Corinthians 10:21).

This booklet could not answer every question or misunderstanding about wine. My intention was to present enough evidence to convince the reader that there are two kinds of wine in Scripture. There is a blessed, nonalcoholic wine (or juice), and a cursed, poisonous, alcoholic wine. It is my prayerful desire that all who read these pages will come to the firm conclusion that Jesus did not make alcoholic wine at the wedding of Cana or offer it to others in the Lord's Supper. Paul did not recommend that Christians drink wine socially or moderately, and neither should Christians today.

The conclusion of the matter is that **Christians should abstain from drinking alcohol** to avoid the unfruitful works of darkness, to allow the devil no room in their lives, to prevent themselves and others from falling, to protect and keep the temple of God from defilement, and to obey God's crucial command to "be sober!" "Wine is a mocker, strong drink is raging: and whosoever is deceived thereby is not wise" (Proverbs 20:1).

Are You A Christian?

I want to thank you for taking the time to read this little book. It has been written for Christians. The title asks, "Should Christians Drink Wine and Alcohol?" I hope that this Bible study has answered that question to your satisfaction. I pray that if you are already a believer who holds the position of abstinence from alcoholic beverages, that this book will strengthen your conviction and resolve. If you have read this book genuinely searching for biblical answers, I pray you too will be edified and come to a firm position of abstinence. If you have Christian friends who believe that social drinking, private drinking, or moderate drinking are fine and acceptable practices, I pray that you might be able to use the biblical principles in this book to convince your friends of the dangers, pitfalls, and poison of alcohol - even if it is consumed in moderation.

This last section of the book is designed to confirm that the reader is indeed a Christian and a child of God. It would be a terrible tragedy if you read this book and decided to quit drinking alcohol, but were cast into the lake of fire on the judgment day because you never received Christ as your Savior. I want you to know and believe four very important Bible truths before closing this book.

1) You are a sinner. I do not state this first truth to be mean or unkind. This is an absolute truth that you must confess if you are to be a child of God. The Bible says, *"There is none righteous, no, not one: . . . For* *all have sinned, and come short of the glory of God"* (Romans 3:10, 23).

What is sin? According to 1 John 3:4, sin is the breaking of God's laws. Most Bible scholars agree that there are more than 600 commands or laws found in just the first five books of the Bible. Many have counted over 1,000 commands in the New Testament. Have you kept all of the laws of God? Can you even name them? Nobody has kept them all. You are a sinner. The sins of an unbeliever have separated him from the thriving, blessed relationship God wants to have with him (Isaiah 59:2).

2) The penalty for sin is death. This truth has been the case throughout human history. When God gave Adam the original rules in the Garden of Eden, God warned Adam that if he sinned and ate the forbidden fruit he would *"surely die"* (Genesis 2:17). The Old Testament prophet Ezekiel confirmed that, *"The soul that sinneth, it shall die"* (Ezekiel 18:20). In the New Testament James wrote, *"and sin, when it is finished, bringeth forth death"* (James 1:15). The Apostle Paul also preached, *"the wages of sin is death"* (Romans 6:23).

The penalty for sin has always been the same. Many churches and religions today have created false doctrines about sin and its penalty. Some churches falsely claim that baptism can wash away sin. Some churches falsely teach that doing good works or keeping a man-made list of sacraments can earn grace and reduce one's time in a fictitious state called purgatory. The Word of God makes no such claims. The Bible says that all unbelieving sinners will face death in the lake of fire forever. This eternal punishment is called *"the second death"* in Revelation 21:8. The bad news is that you are a sinner, and you deserve death in hell-fire forever. However, the good news is very good.

3) Jesus paid the penalty for your sin. Because you are a sinner, and because you could never save yourself, Jesus prepared an amazing way of salvation for you and all people. The Bible teaches that God loves you so much; He does not want you to die in your sins and go to hell. His great love sent Jesus into this world to die and save you from sin's penalty.

The Bible teaches that Jesus laid down His life on the cross to pay the penalty for sin. He was buried, but on the third day He rose from the dead! He proved that only He has power over sin, death, and hell.

Despite the fact that Jesus died and rose for all people, the Bible reveals that most people are *not* on their way to heaven (Matthew 7:13-14). Why? Because the Bible teaches that salvation is a *"gift"* (Romans 6:23; Ephesians 2:8-9). This is too amazing for many people to believe. They have been falsely taught since they were a child that heaven is a place to work for and a place that requires much self-righteousness. In fact, when I ask people if they are sure they will be in heaven someday, the most common answer I hear is "I am trying." Salvation and eternal life with God is not something for which you can work or achieve. Salvation is a free gift that God is offering to you today (1 John 5:13).

4) God wants you to be saved. The Bible says that God is *"not willing that any should perish, but that all should come to repentance"* (2 Peter 3:9). The Bible also teaches that, *"behold, now is the accepted time; behold, now is the day of salvation"* (2 Corinthians 6:2). How can you be saved? How can you become a Christian? **You must repent and receive God's gift of salvation by putting your faith in the Lord Jesus Christ!** You can do this right now. Jesus said, "The time is fulfilled, and the kingdom of God is at hand: repent ye, and believe the gospel"(Mark 1:15). The word Gospel means "good news."

To repent means that one has a change of mind that leads to a change in life direction. Repent **to** the Lord Jesus and **from** your life of sin and self-righteousness today. To become a Christian, you must stop working and trying to earn salvation and you must receive the gift of eternal life by putting your complete trust in Jesus alone to save you from your sin.

Romans 10:9-10 clearly explains how you can become a Christian today. *"That if thou shalt confess with thy mouth the Lord Jesus, and shalt believe in thine heart that God hath raised him from the dead, thou shalt be saved. For with the heart man believeth unto righteousness; and with the mouth confession is made unto salvation."* Would you like to be saved today? Are you willing to confess the four truths above? You are a sinner. The penalty for sin is death. Jesus paid the penalty for your sin. **Repent and believe in the Lord Jesus who died and rose again, and He will save you today!**

Much time and effort has been spent in producing this little book. It would be well worth all the investment just to know that you trusted in the Lord Jesus for your salvation. If you have any questions about this book and its material, or if you have any more questions about salvation and how to become a Christian, please contact us. If you just repented and believed in Christ we would love to hear from you too. We would like to help you in your new life with Christ. We provide free Bibles and discipleship materials for all who are interested.

Please contact us at:
Phone: +(237) 677.02.32.92
Email: Cameroon4Christ@yahoo.com
Mail: P.O. Box: 28 Bambili, Northwest Region, Cameroon Africa

BIBLIOGRAPHY

Aromi. "Guerzoni - Mosto Di Uva." Aromiwineandfood.com. Accessed August 22, 2017. https://aromiwineandfood.com/product/guerzoni-mosto-di-uva--grape-must.

BabyCenter: Expert Advice. "Alcohol and Breastfeeding." Babycenter.com, Accessed June 9, 2018. https://www.babycenter.com/0_alcohol-and-breastfeeding_3547.bc.

Bacchiocchi, Samuele. *Wine in the Bible*. Berrien Springs. MI: Biblical Perspectives, 2001.

Barnes, Albert. *Notes, Explanatory and Practical on the Epistles of Paul to the Thessalonians, to Timothy, to Titus and to Philemon*. New York: Harper & Brothers Publishers, 1873.

Bertelli, A. A. and D. K. Das. "Grapes, Wines, Resveratrol, and Heart Health." National Center for Biotechnical Information. Accessed April 22, 2018. https://www.ncbi.nlm.nih.gov/pubmed/19770673.

Battcock, Mike and Sue Azam-Ali. "Fermented Fruits and Vegtables: A Global Perspective." Food and Agriculture Organization of the United Nations. 1998. Accessed May 14, 2018. http://www.fao.org/docrep/x0560e/x0560e09.htm.

Burton, Robyn and Nick Sheron. "No Level of Alcohol Consumption Improves Health." *The Lancet*. Published online August 23, 2018. Accessed August 28, 2018. https://www.thelancet.com/journals/lancet/article/PIIS0140-6736(18)31571-X/fulltext.

Cato the Elder. *De Agri Cultura*. Translated and published in the Loeb Classical Library, 1934. http://penelope.uchicago.edu/Thayer/E/Roman/Texts/Cato/De_Agricultura/G*.html.

ChemicalSafetyFacts.org. "Ethanol." Accessed May 28, 2018. https://www.chemicalsafetyfacts.org/ethanol/.

Dickens, D. L., H. L. DuPont, and P. C. Johnson. "Survival of Bacterial Enteropathogens in the Ice of Popular Drinks." National Center for Biotechnology Information. Accessed August 22, 2017. https://www.ncbi.nlm.nih.gov/pubmed/3889393.

Doyle, Robin. "What Can I Eat & Drink with a Peptic Ulcer?" Livestrong.com. Accessed August 22, 2017. http://www.livestrong.com/article/340876-what-can-i-eat-drink-with-a-peptic-ulcer/.

Drinkaware. "Is Alcohol Harming Your Stomach?" Drinkaware.com. Accessed August 22, 2017. https://www.drinkaware.co.uk/alcohol-facts/health-effects-of-alcohol/effects-on-the-body/is-alcohol-harming-your-stomach/.

Driscoll, Mark. *The Radical Reformission: Reaching Out Without Selling Out*. Grand Rapids, MI: Zondervan, 2004.

Drummond, Lewis. *Spurgeon: Prince of Preachers*. Grand Rapids, MI: Kregel Publications,1992.

Ewing, Charles Wesley. *The Bible and Its Wines*. Indiana: National Prohibition Foundation, 1985.

Farlex Partner Medical Dictionary. "Inspissation." The Free Dictionary. Accessed August 22, 2017. http://medical-dictionary.thefreedictionary.com/inspissation.

Farrar, Cannon. "Wine." in *Smith's Bible Dictionary*. ed. William Smith. Grand Rapids, MI: A.J. Holman, 1884.

Gakidou, Emmanuela and Global Burden of Disease 2016 Alcohol Collaborators. "Alcohol Use and Burden for 195 Countries and Territories, 1990–2016: A Systematic Analysis for the Global Burden of Disease Study 2016." *The Lancet*. Published online August 23, 2018. Accessed August 28, 2018. https://www.thelancet.com/action/showPdf?pii=S0140-6736%2818%2931310-2.

Google. "Liquor." Google Dictionary. Accessed August 22, 2017. https://www.google.com/search?q=liquor+definition&oq=liquor+definition&aqs=chrome.0.69i59j0l5.4590j0j7&sourceid=chrome&ie=UTF-8.

_____. "Wine." Google Dictionary. Accessed August 22, 2017. https://www.google.com/search?q=wine+definition&oq=wine+definition&aqs=chrome..69i57j0l5.2311j0j7&sourceid=chrome&ie=UTF-8.

Hamilton, Frank. *Extracts by Frank Hamilton from The Bible Wine by the late Ferrar Fenton*. London: A. & C. Black, Ltd. 1938.

Henard, William D. and Adam W. Greenway. *Evangelicals Engaging Emergent: A Discussion of the Emergent Church Movement*. Nashville, TN: B&H Publishing Group, 2009.

Hirsch, Emil G. and Judah David Eisenstein. "Wine." JewishEncyclopedia.com. Accessed August 22, 2017. http://jewishencyclopedia.com/articles/14941-wine.

Hughes, R. Kent. *Romans: Righteousness From Heaven*. Wheaton, IL: Crossway, 1991.

Ironside, H. A. *1 and 2 Timothy, Titus, and Philemon*. Grand Rapids, MI: Kregel, 2008.

Jaeggli, Randy. *Christians and Alcohol: A Scriptural Case for Abstinence*. Greenville, SC: Bob Jones University Press, 2014.

Kent, Homer Jr. *The Pastoral Epistles*. Winona Lake, IN: BMH Books, 1995.

Kulp, Joshua Kulp. "Terumot, Chapter Two, Mishnah Six." SHIURIM. Accessed August 22, 2017. http://learn.conservativeyeshiva.org/terumot-chapter-two-mishnah-six/.

Lees, Frederic Richard and Dawson Burns. *The Temperance Bible-Commentary*. London: S. W. Partridge, 1868.

Lukacas, Paul. *Inventing Wine: A New History Of One Of The World's Most Ancient Pleasures*. New York: W. W. Norton & Company, Inc. 2012.

MacArthur, John MacArthur. *The Superiority of Christ*. Chicago, IL: Moody Press, 1986.

Malconson, Keith. *Sober Saints: Should Christians Drink Alcohol?* n/a: Heaven Sent Revival Publishing, 2013.

Matthews-King, Alex. "Glass Of Wine A Day Could Shave Years Off Your Life Warns Study Calling For Global Reduction Of Alcoholic Limits." Independent.co.uk. Accessed April 21, 2018. https://www.independent.co.uk/news/health/alcohol-death-drinking-life-expectancy-safe-limits-reduced-beer-wine-pint-glass-cambridge-a8301876.html.

McGee, J. Vernon. *First and Second Timothy/Titus/Philemon*. Nashville, TN: Thomas Nelson Inc., 1991.

Mfunywi, Eugine. Interview by Ben David Sinclair. Bambili, Cameroon. June 7, 2018.

Moi University. Course Notes, PS 2843 "Bible-Wines." Course Hero. Accessed August 22, 2017. https://www.coursehero.com/file/p3p88f6/The-art-of-distillation-was-then-unknown-it-was-not-discovered-till-the-ninth/.

National Institute on Alcohol Abuse and Alcoholism. "Alcohol's Effects on the Body." NIAAA.nih.gov. Accessed April 23, 2018. https://www.niaaa.nih.gov/alcohol-health/alcohols-effects-body.

Patton, William Patton. *Bible Wines*. New York: National Temperance Society, 1874.

Philips, Edward. "The New World of English Words." Internet Archive. Accessed August 22, 2017. https://archive.org/stream/The_New_World_of_English_Words_Or_A_General_Dictionary#page/n707/mode/2up/search/wine.

Phillips, John. *Exploring the Pastoral Epistles*. Grand Rapids, MI: Kregel, 2004.

Reinagel, Monica. "Myths about Sulfites and Wine." Scientific American. July 15, 2017. Accessed May 28, 2018. https://www.scientificamerican.com/article/myths-about-sulfites-and-wine/.

Robinson, Jancis. *The Oxford Companion to Wine*. 3rd ed. Oxford University Press, 2006.

Simpson, John. "The First Dictionaries of English." Oxford English Dictionary. http://public.oed.com/aspects-of-english/english-in-time/the-first-dictionaries-of-english/. Accessed August 22, 2017.

Sinclair, Ben. *Spiritual Growth Series*. Bamenda, Cameroon: Gospel Press, 2010.

Spurgeon, Charles. *C. H. Spurgeon's Autobiography*. London: Passmore and Alabaster, 1900.

Strong, James. "G3525: νήφω nḗphō." Blue Letter Bible. Accessed August 22, 2017. https://www.blueletterbible.org/lang/lexicon/lexicon.cfm?Strongs=G3525&t=KJV&ss=1.

Teachout, Richard. *Grape Juice in the Bible: God's Blessing for His People!* Quebec Canada: Etude Biblique pour Aujourd'hui, 2011.

Trench, Richard Chenevix. *Miracles of Our Lord*. London: D. Appleton and Company.

Ukpaka, Chukwuemeka Peter. "Studying Fermentation Characteristics of Some Palm Wine Obtained in Niger Delta Area of Nigeria." *International Journal of Novel Research in Engineering & Pharmaceutical Sciences*. Volume 1, Issue 2 (Spring 2014): 1.

United States Environmental Protection Agency. "The History of Drinking Water Treatment." EPA. Accessed May 28, 2018. http://esa21.kennesaw.edu/modules/water/drink-water-trt/drink-water-trt-hist-epa.pdf.

Vatican. "Chapter III: The Proper Celebration Of Mass." Congregation for Divine Worship and the Discipline of the Sacrament. Accessed August 22, 2017. http://www.vatican.va/roman_curia/congregations/ccdds/documents/rc_con_ccdds_doc_20040423_redemptionis-sacramentum_en.html#Chapter III.

Vine, William Edwy. "B-1 Verb Strong's Number: G3525." Blue Letter Bible. Accessed August 22, 2017. https://www.blueletterbible.org/search/Dictionary/viewTopic.cfm?topic=VT0002682.

Watson, D. F. "Wine." in *Dictionary of Jesus and the Gospels: A Compendium of Contemporary Biblical Scholarship*. ed. Joel B. Green and Scot McKnight. Downers Grove, IL: InterVarsity Press, 1992.

WebMD. "Fainting Treatment." Webmd.com. Accessed August 22, 2017. http://www.webmd.com/first-aid/fainting-treatment.

_____. "The Buzz about Grape Juice." WebMD.com. Accessed August 22, 2017. http://www.webmd.com/food-recipes/features/buzz-about-grape-juice#1.

_____. "What Is Peptic Ulcer Disease?" WebMD.com. Accessed August 22, 2017. http://www.webmd.com/digestivedisorders/digestive-diseases-peptic-ulcer-disease#1.

Welch's. "Our History." Welchs.com. Accessed August 22, 2017. http://www.welchs.com/about-us/our-story/our-history.

Whittington, Brad. *What Would Jesus Drink?* Austin, Texas: Wunderfool Press, 2011.

Wood, Angela M. & About 120 Other Doctors and Scientist. "Risk Thresholds For Alcohol Consumption: Combined Analysis Of Individual-Participant Data For 599,912 Current Drinkers In 83 Prospective Studies." *The Lancet*, Volume 391, Number 10129: 1455- 1548. Accessed April 22, 2018. http://www.thelancet.com/journals/lancet/article/PIIS0140-6736(18)30134-X/fulltext.

20534936R00033

Made in the USA
Lexington, KY
05 December 2018